The Essence of Life

CW01426053

Hira Gul

BookLeaf
Publishing

India | USA | UK

The Essence of Life © 2023 Hira Gul

All rights reserved.

Presentation by *BookLeaf Publishing*

Web: www.bookleafpub.com

E-mail: info@bookleafpub.com

ISBN: 9789358317244

First edition 2023

To my beloved husband Smaak, you are the unwavering support, the muse of my heart, and the endless love story that fills the pages of my life. This book is dedicated to you with all my love.

ACKNOWLEDGEMENT

I would like to thank my family for willingly reading my poems and constantly supporting my creativity. Special credit goes to my beloved husband whose encouragement I could not do without.

Most of all, I would like to thank BookLeaf Publishing for giving me the opportunity to publish a book, which has been a lifelong dream of mine. Without you, this compilation would not exist.

PREFACE

Poetry is the essence of life, capturing specific
moments that induce happiness or pain. Writing
is a form of acknowledging your fate, and
succumbing to your destiny. The power of the
pen combined with the power of the mind is
completely capable of producing uncontrollable
wonders. The eyes bear witness and testify for
the product they see, in awe of the complex
emotions hidden behind a façade of disjointed
language; language that strings together,
formulating new connections and meanings in a
world of false connections.

The Golden Hours

The days are dying, you say one morning
you're not exactly lying either...
the stench of decay emanates from one street to
the next
as darkness engulfs all: broken streetlights
hinder illumination
and you're constantly submerged in the
unknown.

But the crunching beneath your feet remains
satisfying
though a far enjoyable experience when you can
witness
an array of the entire spectrum:
golds amidst the almost-forgotten greens;
the vibrant orange and red which beautify all
walks of daily life.

You remember leaping into the crunchy palette
surprising your sibling with a fistful aimed at
their head
persistently chasing each other, the sun
descending on your shadows.
Now some prepare to burrow away in the
coming weeks

whilst others keep treading forwards incessantly.

You are far too focused on the memories of here
and now though
valuing the present, immersed in the splashes of
colour splayed out before you.
Yet anticipation along with frustration lingers
that days are becoming futile
blurring into one deep undistinguishable void
so, you remind yourself you couldn't care less -
it's about time to stop feeling pitiful.

From Words to Pain

Disputes arise as a result of miscommunication.
One misunderstands, the other ignores
whilst someone misleads
complete disagreement in which everyone
believes
they are right
and that the opposition should be supportive
of their one-dimensional perspective,
but the truth is unclear
a translucent string of letters.

Opposition strikes
complete contradictions bordering on
exaggeration
false accusations
back and forth, an endless tirade.

Today is the Same as Yesterday

The air is cool, numbs fingertips
a reminder that she is outdoors
for in her reverie, she is lost
until the moment she almost slips
about to land face-first but is somehow
saved by a miracle, a gust of wind
that chills her down to her soul
penetrating through thick woolly layers:
a sudden thought that she is not alone prevails.
After all, in her heart it all replays
endlessly like a broken record
a chain of memories far too intense
to forget, abandon, leave behind forever.
So she waits for the perfect opportunity
(that may never arise at all, but you never know)
patience a virtue she's learnt the hard way
still waiting to begin again.

Mischief

Swooping down, they approached their territory
signalling to the others they had returned.
Immediately, they were ambushed
for prized possessions everyone longed for.

Tearing at seeds with their beaks,
a new dispute had arisen-
the elderly attempted to pacify the youngsters
who were too feisty for their liking.
But peace had been disrupted
and would not return for a long time,
or at least not until the feast disappeared,

and then another squabble would replace it-
this time over whose responsibility
it would be to take care of the newly laid
waiting for their hatching-
and nobody, absolutely nobody
wanted that responsibility.

Deeper Than Depths

The water is calm, cool to the fingertips
serenity glimmering
gentle ripples, flowing waves
clearing her mind, she watches
mesmerised by the constancy, the cyclical nature
of the once overflowing memories.
Though now at ease, they tease
the brim of her hat
peep out to the sea where they dive
and swim,
before eventually sinking
dissolving into salt, leaving no traces
but the water and the girl
still watching
still thinking
still sorry.

Your Mood Defines You

The essence of happiness cannot be grasped
it lingers, free from judgement
hopeful after trying times
its purpose a form of escapism.

Incomprehensible excitement
sourcing from the heart and reaching
out to those you meet, greet and interact with.

Smiles are contagious, where joy begins
the only evidence of ecstasy
though short-lived, in its passing
you remain thankful for your blessings.

The End of it All

Nostalgia swept me away momentarily
the humming wind embraced me
initially it was soothing
but then I was stifled in an oppressive void
gasping for breath as I desperately demanded
release.

It was only instances later I was free from its
influence
lying slack, trembling uncontrollably

there and then I knew I didn't want to endure
anymore
complete hopelessness paired with helplessness
struck my mind.

Looking down at my lifeless form far below
I swooped down, grasping my icy hands
a shudder overcame me
and I knew that I was no more
for I had already decided the ending.

Tomorrow is the Same as Today

They expect her to be busy
constantly hustling, moving, travelling
striving after achievements like they grow on
trees
can simply be reached within grasp
tugged free from stubborn branches at ease
into her pocket, a token to commemorate
it all.

She hates expectations though
only doing what others expect of her:
rigid, confined, impenetrable.
So she discloses little to those around her
acting on whims and impulses to her heart's
content
little does she know they know it all,
feign ignorance as it's easier to remain silent
and accept she cannot be tethered down
imprisoned forever.
One day they will have to let her go
she will gladly leave it all behind and begin her
own journey for real this time.

Deception at its Finest

Gasping for air, she clung to the branch
holding on for dear life
aware that in those last moments
all hope was futile
and her fate was inescapable.

I watched her struggle,
her writhing pathetic form
fumbling for her missing inhaler
which I had destroyed minutes earlier
not that she knew I'd done it…

She deserved it though.
after all, it was her fault we were lost
starved, desperate, feverish
with sickness emanating from our breaths
all because of her sheer stupidity
I'd blindly followed her.

I knew that my time was also coming
but I would never give her the satisfaction
of outliving me. Never.
So here it comes:
her pitiful accidental end
with absolutely no one to blame
besides herself.

In the end, we only regret the chances we didn't take

The beautiful lie ruined his life
there was no remedy for his inner strife
he sank deeper
until he could go no further
but it was too late
to begin to hate, or even contemplate
how to save himself.

He had grown to cherish
the unimaginable
the inconceivable
but regardless, the impossible.

The forgery of the mind
encompassed everything in sight
so it was unsurprising that he was trapped
for he was undeniably wrapped-
tethered to the being
who he couldn't stop seeing
as his destiny, his life.

She witnessed his every move
willing to attest and prove
from the day he was lured in

to how he was presently submerged within
a foolish fantasy.

Physically restraining herself, she merely
watched
his descent, wishing she'd intervened
at an earlier stage.
Yet she hadn't been able to control her rage
so instead detached her own emotions
altering the absurd versions
of the future she'd envisioned for herself

pity continued to linger
his state the obvious trigger
though he would never know that he was the
cause
of it all.

But most of all, she envied him
as her world had become so dim
whilst his was ignited, blooming
with the tendrils of first love.
His ecstasy was her pain
her loss was his gain

eventually, she was forced to give up
leaving what remained of her desire behind her
and she concealed her frustration
appearing to be in peace

but so utterly out of reach to those around her.

Happiness will always exceed the pain
he was happy for many more years
his every wish fulfilled at the touch of his
fingertips.

She vanished and was never heard from again
but her presence lingered for eternity- envy.

Fate

The reflection speaks
lures him closer, seduces with promises
of prosperity and limitless bounties; an
eternity of blissful contentment
a fulfilment of transgressive desires
followed by an appreciation of the
blessed beauty of the world

manifested in his reflection,
a flawless nature apparent
no loss, no fault, no indication

of the unfortunate tragedy that will befall him
written in the stars, awaiting to come into
existence.
That twilight, he shall undoubtedly perish
for his sins
as the reflection devours all

ultimately prevailing in the hands of corruption
his other self longing to wreak havoc
amongst the silence, leaving no trace
of a once enviable soul.

Now, the flower, the namesake
is submerged in a pool of water (a pitiful
replacement)
lacking in all aspects of beauty

purer than he ever was, dainty and vulnerable
against the oppressive tide longing to destroy the
lasting remnants
sinking slowly, then swallowed by waves-
no longer a replacement, suffering the same end.
A mirror, a replication, a reflection of his final
moment.

He sank, it sank, they sank.
One and the same.

Narcissus.

The Nature of Inspiration

*Inspiration: noun, the process of being mentally
stimulated to do or feel something, especially to
do something creative.*

Begins as a figment of the imagination
an isolated thought

submerged within the depths of what is daily
sought
a dwelling in the near-distant future

yet when it comes to that specific moment
you seek to capture

long to imprison on paper and transfer from the
mind
words will always unknowingly slip from grasp

fall straight through beckoning hands- gone.
Though the candle was once lit

the short-lived warmth has dispersed
any testing thoughts have dissipated

as though forced to retreat
unwilling to become an immediate means of
correspondence

now impossible to determine
it's a pity such moments of inspiration prefer to
remain lost.

Being concealed in forlorn depths
requires an attempt to summon from a peculiar
bubble

in order to release non-sensical words and letters
that can only be described as thought-provoking

instigating an immediate notice
diverting attention from the world

to the intricacies of language
and the unexpected influence of the
subconscious.

What is the purpose of these random words, you
may ask?
Their existence is reflective of the complex
nature

of a ponderous mind
and the making of the indefinite process of art.

Finally, when it's time to commence
you can wholly appreciate that you have found
your muse

though how you found it you'll never really
know
as it was previously buried within the confining
tunnel

of what is known as memory
once having deviated from invitation

now the freedom of words on a page reflects a
continuation
of a train of thought- the endless journey of the
unforgivable process.

Destruction

Tremors of ice shatter all that is in sight
foundations shudder, thrusting to the left and
right
from the intense abruptness of the impact

they watch, mesmerised by the gradual change
the descent from grandness to futility, a relapse

rubble crumbles. A scream. An arm beneath the
debris reaching out
accompanied by a shout. An echo. Another
scream followed by further chaos.

Then the deafening silence of suffering.
An everlasting reminder of the tragedy
damaging their lives forever.

30.04.19

It is known that people find peace in nature
(true enough in short moments):
immersed in their surroundings
wafts of breeze accompanied by intervals of
sunshine,
bouts of hay fever – the occasional sneeze,
tickly pollen in the air – becoming the biggest
irritant.
Chased by bees along with spiders crawling on
their head,
awaiting the verdict on their life
that will inevitably follow.
Crows on a midday walk with leftover picnic
stuffed in their beaks – a typical day.
Yet it's the last day of April.

In the midst of moments of reflection
the memory of the spider I killed yesterday
plagues on my mind
(the same spider that incidentally was on my
head)
meanwhile, sitting on a bench
I tell myself I'm just thinking
for how much longer this will possibly last
and it works.

True Identity

It can only be described as timeless
a prolonged expanse of nothingness
with individual memories holding little
significance
but the overall picture incomplete
without the smallest of intricacies:
moments of excitement
followed by those of pain.

It would be the same anywhere
here or there,
nonetheless there remains a sense of belonging
in this foreign land
people across the world call home.

For Now

Petals drift, float like bubbles,
fluttering through the air-
an epitome of beauty, delicacy,
undeniably fragile.

Their purpose creates clarity
of the passage of time
as inevitably it is the beginning
of new experiences:
rebirth after the transition
from confinement, the darkness that overwhelms
to tender sun-lit months.

Streets are paved with what remains of the
tendrils
serving as an everlasting photograph
of gradual change. The shifting
trails along with wafts of breeze
are a sign that warmth is yet to come.

Seeking Salvation

I used to believe in eternity
but nothing lasts forever, least of all time.
The devouring emptiness consumes the fire
whilst the entirety of anatomy dissipates into
fury,
an endless train of loss.

Confusion, shock and sympathy-
any attempt to empathise is inadequate
cannot bring justice
since ultimately I am unable to accept
misfortune.

Finally, when reality attacks, I realise it's over,
intent to reminisce the final traces of moments
I never knew would hold such significance.
Yet the inevitability of no more again
along with the impossibility to resume what has
passed
or mend fractured ties renders the conclusion
that time allows no sense of closure.

Trials and tribulations remain brutal
as does separation;
harsh criticisms verge on the intrusive

infringe the boundary between guilt and
accountability.
I am neither entitled to freedom nor captivity
however, I exist, am present.

Is it possible to redeem what has passed,
attain acceptance of past mistakes
and encourage growth
from this point onwards?

Line by Line

Only described as words on a page

a continuation of a train of thought-

an endless journey.

Thought-provoking, forced to acknowledge,

notice the intricacies,

their possible purpose.

A reason for their existence, reflective of

the complex nature of a poet's mind

remains evident on the page.

Survive

Ending is always hard

broken goodbyes,

a detachment from reality

filled with sorrow.

There is only despair

followed by devastation

an inability to leave behind

and move on to resume life.

Then follows nostalgia,

an intense longing to return

but one can only reminisce

and await should the opportunity arise.

Cool Warmth

The pelting rain is a swarm of ice
bites on exposed skin, gnaws on bones
a tickle, as we laugh uncontrollably
though tremble with each gust of wind
shuddering violently as hair is plastered to scalp.

Bright patches of light appear
soon disappearing behind the clouds
once more. The short-lived heat
is comforting, a light bulb
that fused too soon.

But in its place are stripes,
so faint that we almost miss them
a thin arch stretching as wide as can be seen.
We squint in the midst of the shower
making a wish for more joy.

The Masterpiece

Dusty hues illuminate the sky
an artist's palette of vibrant shades
slowly sinking, stripes dripping
down the canvas

darkness follows
engulfing the entirety of creation
and submerges the painting
in glowing moonlight

speckles of glittering satellites
are scattered like fine droplets
the perfect finishing touch
capturing time and place in that instant

an unimaginable, yet ethereal sight.

9 789358 317244